What do you call a good story?

A mind reliever.
A page-turner.
A rewind.
A laughing, crying fit.

Write to Keep On Crying (TEARS!): 300-Plus Writing Story Prompts for a Laugh-Out-Loud Comedy Novel, Screenplay, or Stageplay
Copyright (c) 2023 Hakeela Buford / AF.FORD MEDIA, LLC

For information:
AF.FORD MEDIA, LLC
15826 S La Grange Road, Ste. 265
Orland Park, IL 60462
www.affordmedia.co

BOOKS
An Imprint Division of AF.FORD MEDIA, LLC

Printed in the United States of America

ISBN 979-8-9852114-6-7 (print)   ISBN 979-8-9852114-7-4 (ebook)

Book Design By AF.FORD MEDIA, LLC
Courteous credits to Gabrielle Henderson on Unsplash for cover photography

Write to Keep on Crying
(TEARS!)

**300+ Writing Story Prompts
for a
Laugh-Out-Loud Comedy
Novel, Screenplay, or Stageplay**

Hakeela Buford

BOOKS

To all of the ~~true~~ comedians in our lives

who make us cry

but in a good way

INTRODUCTION

What this book is not is a route.
It's a driver's seat.

What it isn't is a trope
(although we all like a good one
every now and then).
It's an audience awaiting your plot
twists.

It's purely just a set-up
for your own punchline.

And if the world is also just a stage,
you're about to make it
the most entertaining one yet.
So, let's open the curtains
and your creative mind
and its unique brand of humor
to pull out all of the stops

and keep us crying.

THE SET-UP
Love is in the air

The meanest person you've ever known, the sweetest person you've ever known, and the most neutral person you've ever known. Put together in one room. High levels of dopamine and norepinephrine released in an invisible mist.

THE PUNCHLINE
What happens next?

THE SET-UP
People, places, & things

Make 3 lists, 3 items in each. The first list is all people, the second list is all places, the last list is all things. Now, switch them up: people becoming places, places becoming things, and things becoming people.

THE PUNCHLINE

Which exactly have you switched, and why have you done it you sick, twisted person?

THE SET-UP
Tooth for a tooth

A vain dentist who is known as a serial ----boy comes up against the wrong woman...a Louisiana-bred woman he dumps who then sets a plan into motion.
For every woman he's ever scorned, there goes a tooth.

THE PUNCHLINE
What happens to the doctor's fate?

THE SET-UP
Baby fever/And if you don't know,
now you know/You ARE the baby('s father/daddy)

An everlasting bachelor wakes up in the body of a baby...The son he never knew he had.

But now he does.

THE PUNCHLINE
How will he return to his normal self?

THE SET-UP
The bare essentials

Four body parts. One of 'em's got to go. But what? But HOW?

And what happens when one of 'em incites all of 'em to partake in a revolt for being discarded as unessential?

THE PUNCHLINE

THE SET-UP
What is it good for? Absolutely something.
A.K.A. Making somethin' out of nuthin'

A 21st century disgruntled boomer decides to start a viral trend and channel doing absolutely nothing to stick it to The Man of today's age. Until The Man, the social influencers, come knocking at his door. For collabos.

THE PUNCHLINE
What happens now?

When a magic worker kidnaps a popular, attractive social influencer and forces them to trade spots, the worker doesn't realize the social influencer is a magician too...or knows some good magicians.

The social influencer warns the worker about repercussions if they don't switch back. The worker ignores it, until one day, the earth moves in between the moon and sun, blocking the light from the sun...and creating a shadow. One that reveals the worker's true self.

THE PUNCHLINE

THE SET-UP

No goodwill

Santa Claus.
Inflation.
Goodwill (or eBay or garage sale)

THE PUNCHLINE

Where is this story going? What is going on with Santa?

THE SET-UP

Santa's clause

When one social influencer insults with too many rants in the eyes and minds of his grandkids', Santa takes matters into his own hands.

THE PUNCHLINE

What kind of proverbial bag of coal will take place?

THE SET-UP

Opening Scene: car rental site
Main Character: plumber
Items: Jet ski, will & testament, cell phone, vending machine

THE PUNCHLINE

"Did you check the bag of Doritos?!!"

Yep, we're as confused as you are about what's going on here. It's your job to make us less confused and more amused.

THE SET-UP

No goodwill pt. 2

Inflation times call for inflation measures.
After becoming short on paying his North Pole property taxes, Santa treats himself this Christmas...with bitcoins stolen from his Christmas address book.

THE PUNCHLINE

Yeah, he's coming down the chimneys this Christmas.But it definitely isn't for delivering presents.

THE SET-UP

We won't laugh (at you). Promise.

Think of the most horrible thing that's ever happened to you. Then change the names in the story. Then tell us.

THE PUNCHLINE

THE SET-UP
Sleeping Not So Beautifully

Sleeping Beauty hits menopause.

THE PUNCHLINE
Honestly, that was it above. But see how you can make it even more ridiculous and (comically) unfortunate.

THE SET-UP

"Tell me...What was the reason for leaving your last job?"

THE PUNCHLINE
"It's kind of a (not so) funny story..."

THE SET-UP
Now You See It. Now You Don't.

A job interview goes terribly wrong, terribly fast.

THE PUNCHLINE
And somehow, it involves: A flat-belly tea. A psychic. A correctional officer.

THE SET-UP
It sells itself (into disaster)

A con man who recently has lost his memory desperately seeks life insurance from a broker who remembers it all.

THE PUNCHLINE
Including the fact that the man once conned him.

THE SET-UP

"So, I'm at the bar. And in walks a..."

THE PUNCHLINE

The last thing you ate.
The last thing on earth you'd ever eat.
The most recent song lyrics you heard.
The last person things got weird with.
Make us laugh.

THE SET-UP
Dad, Jokes (on You)

A man who just can't seem to ever take things seriously is left by his family at a resort during a winter storm after taking it too far in his comedy set.

THE PUNCHLINE
What happened before? What happens next?

THE SET-UP

"'It will be fun,' they said."

THE PUNCHLINE

Nintendo. Tax filing. Mistaken identity.
Make us have fun; make us laugh.

THE SET-UP

"How can you be laughing at a time like this?!"

THE PUNCHLINE

"Well, actually...For a couple of reasons..."

THE SET-UP

"...
Well...that went left."

THE PUNCHLINE

Explain what just happened.

THE SET-UP

A desparate job seeker suddenly works under the weather.

Literally.

THE PUNCHLINE

"But there's seven inches of snow outside!"
"I know. I caused it. Now, report to the office."

THE SET-UP
Take it with a pinch of salt.

A pinch of salt.
A taker.
A situation.
A whole lot of salt. The whole container.
A sudden wild change of events.

THE PUNCHLINE

THE SET-UP

"Where do you see yourself in five years?"

"It sure in the heck won't be here."

THE PUNCHLINE
Where the heck are you? And where the heck are you going???
Take us with you!

THE SET-UP

"What did you like most about your last position?"

THE PUNCHLINE

"The way my boss's face looked when I walked out."

THE SET-UP

"Can you tell me about a stressful work situation and how you overcame it?"

THE PUNCHLINE

Detergent.
Gummy candy.
A kid who has accidentally
swallowed a block toy.
How does this relate to work?

THE SET-UP

Not exactly skeletons in the closet

"Whatever you do,...DON'T go in that closet."

THE PUNCHLINE

So, naturally, we do.
And find: Barbies. One of the dead presidents. That ONE item we've been looking for for years (NOT including our unpaired socks from mysterious dryer runs).

THE SET-UP
Freddy Krueger, WHO??

> "Whatever you do,...DON'T fall asleep."

THE PUNCHLINE

So, naturally, we do.
And...
Oh boy.
This isn't good.

THE SET-UP
There's no bigger threat than living paycheck to paycheck.

> "YOU'RE GONNA PAY FOR THIS!!!"

THE PUNCHLINE
"Yeah. Welcome to capitalism. Glad you could join us."

THE SET-UP

WHO: The career, of the last person you talked to, becoming a character
WHAT: The silliest thing you feared as a kid
WHEN: The end of the world
WHERE: The place of the worst timing you ever had or witnessed
HOW: The last action you saw in person, on social media, or on the internet and cringed at

THE PUNCHLINE
This should be interesting.

"Where'd you get this from anyway??"

THE PUNCHLINE

...
"Tricky."

THE SET-UP

"Now, SOMEbody's! lyin'."

THE PUNCHLINE

"Uh-oh. Who's lyin'??"
And what is their impending fate?

THE SET-UP
What's (Really) Goin' On?

"So, uh...
What's going on over there?"

"...What are you talking about?"

THE PUNCHLINE
"Unh-*huh*.
*Some*thing's going on."

THE SET-UP

"Hey, you have five dollars I can borrow until next week when I get paid?"

THE PUNCHLINE
"Oh, baby, I wish I did. I'd throw you down and make you take it."

THE SET-UP

"What was wrong with the last guy *this* time?"

THE PUNCHLINE
"Everything."

THE SET-UP

Tell the story of this person's latest terrible date.

"If a tree falls in the forest and there's no one around to hear it, does it make a sound?"

THE PUNCHLINE
"Probably not.
But if the tree falls on a campfire in that forest, the town sure will."

THE SET-UP

After not getting the chance to as a child, a thirty-year-old woman decides she's going to give herself the chance now.

THE PUNCHLINE

She's going to become a ballerina.

THE SET-UP

One day, suddenly, only animals can talk.

THE PUNCHLINE

THE SET-UP

One day, suddenly, women can only talk through cooking and cleaning.

THE PUNCHLINE

And if the guys thought this was all their biggest dreams come true, what they don't know is...

THE SET-UP

All someone wants to do is get home. But it seems like everything is working against them.

THE PUNCHLINE

What happens?
Then what?
And THEN what?

THE SET-UP

Someone (unsuccessfully) tries to ruin their blind date.

THE PUNCHLINE

THE SET-UP

Someone takes a job interview as a joke, thinking they won't get it.

THE PUNCHLINE

Looks like joke's on them.
And it's not your simple data entry or business role; let's just put it like that.

THE SET-UP

A job interview turns out not to be as advertised
and is something very, very different and bizarre.

THE PUNCHLINE

What is the interview *really?*

THE SET-UP

Just when the day couldn't get worse, it does.

THE PUNCHLINE

THE SET-UP

"So...who's gonna tell him?"

THE PUNCHLINE

Yeah, who does? Tell us. But challenge: It's not what's told
but how it's told that will send us over the edge.

THE SET-UP

Spell check comes to life.

THE PUNCHLINE
And yes, things get just as ridiculous and petty as this all sounds.

THE SET-UP

"The human ate my homework."

THE PUNCHLINE
Explain. NOW.

THE SET-UP

He didn't listen to that last part.

THE PUNCHLINE

...Oh boy.

THE SET-UP

A person goes outside to get a mailed package and finds two kangaroos fighting in the middle of the street.

THE PUNCHLINE

THE SET-UP

An obsessed archeologist comes across the last (and unknown) member of the dinosaur species...

THE PUNCHLINE

And...well... It's not exactly as expected.

THE SET-UP

A couple mutually forgets their anniversary, then, suspecting the other is planning revenge, spend the following days internally panicking about how to apologize to the other.

THE PUNCHLINE

Both of their plans COMPLETELY backfire when...

THE SET-UP

One door closes and another opens.

THE PUNCHLINE

Except for one guy, even with loads of money behind it, it just opens the door to more unfortunate events. Turns out the money belongs to one pissed off kid entrepreneur.

THE SET-UP

A guy who attends strangers' funerals goes to one where there is an urn rather than a casket and realizes he's just attended his own:
The deceased man looks just like him, and the family is certain he has risen from the dead (or ashes).

THE PUNCHLINE

Good. Because he owes them...

THE SET-UP

When a mom takes one day too long to repay her daughter five bucks from the hard-earned lemonade stand job she set up over the summer, the daughter has to teach mommy a lesson.

THE PUNCHLINE

So, she puts her mother on...
Time-out? Punishment? Probation???

THE SET-UP

A father hands over a slip of paper that reads "PTO Request" to his bosses: his two-month-old and two-year-old.

THE PUNCHLINE

THE SET-UP

Two kids in a spelling bee are acting like they're playing for money and the whole school year off from homework rather than just the plastic trophy they'll be getting.

THE PUNCHLINE

None of the school staff has the heart to tell them that along with the homework they still have, they also...

THE SET-UP

After one night of ABCs too many, a kindergartener decides they're quitting elementary school and going to...

THE PUNCHLINE

THE SET-UP

Two people at a court trial somehow end up engaging in a prolonged match of the staring game.

THE PUNCHLINE

One of the two people is...

THE SET-UP

Two people at a doctor's office somehow end up engaging in a prolonged match of the staring game.

THE PUNCHLINE

The two people are...

THE SET-UP

Two people on a public transit somehow end up engaging in a prolonged match of the staring game.

THE PUNCHLINE

One of the two people is...

Someone blows a dog whistle, and it brings all of the dogs to the yard...

THE PUNCHLINE

...and a _____.

Someone sneezes, and a person puts a Voodoo spell on them instead of blessing them.

THE PUNCHLINE

Tic-tac-toe between a niece and her uncle goes from fun to full-out competition.

THE PUNCHLINE

THE SET-UP

A teacher walks in on a student forging their parent's signature.

THE PUNCHLINE

Ah, well...Gotta be quicker than that. BUT the kid has a good excuse...

THE SET-UP

A man sprints by, a group of kids after his tail.

THE PUNCHLINE

No, his literal tail.

THE SET-UP

A grandparent educates his grandkid on vinyl records.

THE PUNCHLINE

THE SET-UP

Someone in the store buys all of their fruits and vegetables on the specific day mentioned as Best By date, believing that is when they get ripe.

THE PUNCHLINE

...Who's going to tell them before the huge mistake? Do they go home, whip up lunch, and...?? What then?

THE SET-UP

A stroll on a sidewalk and up comes a tied-up set of parents with a "For Sale" sign taped on them.

THE PUNCHLINE

THE SET-UP

Various generational slangs become true foreign languages.

THE PUNCHLINE

So, needless to say, when a grandchild tries to warn their grandparent of an incoming stampede of geese....Yeah.

THE SET-UP

A stroll on a sidewalk and up comes a tied-up baby with a sign taped on:
"Oops. Did it again."

THE PUNCHLINE

What did the baby do? Again?
And why was it enough to be tied?

THE SET-UP

Man's best friend no more

A stroll on a sidewalk and up comes a tied-up dog with a sign taped on that says:

"Oops. Did it again."

THE PUNCHLINE

What did the dog do? Again?
Challenge: Can't be messing up furniture or clothes.

THE SET-UP

It's a bird. It's a plane!

THE PUNCHLINE

No.
Actually, it's a....

THE SET-UP

Goldilocks gets more than she bargained for when she tries the bears' porridge.

THE PUNCHLINE

No wonder she's sleepy. Turns out the porridge is actually...

THE SET-UP

"You look like a car with no warranty."

THE PUNCHLINE

What's the comeback? Where is this happening, and exactly WHAT is happening?

THE SET-UP

If you can't beat them, join one.

"You can't fire me. I'm your MOTHER!"

A group of stay-at-home moms have had enough and start a national movement to get unionized.

THE PUNCHLINE

In retaliation, their kids do the same. Then seeing all of the benefits that are better than their 9-to-5s, the fathers take a stand.

THE SET-UP

A day goes from weird to weirder.

THE PUNCHLINE

THE SET-UP

Adults worldwide form a union for working parents, going on strike. This forces all non-adult children to work.

THE PUNCHLINE

Not going for it, the children...

THE SET-UP

Knowing that the precocious kid next door is spying on them once again, the neighbors decide to give the little conniver the experience of a lifetime and act like...

THE PUNCHLINE

THE SET-UP

"Do you want fries with that?"

THE PUNCHLINE

"Yes, please. And if you could drop this week's winning lotto numbers in there, too, that would be great. Thanks."

THE SET-UP

"How old are you?"

THE PUNCHLINE

"Too old to be asked that. I'll tell you that much."

THE SET-UP

The "Over It" Millennials and Gen Zers

"What is your greatest strength?"

THE PUNCHLINE

"Getting paid what I'm worth or getting another interview with your competitor."

THE SET-UP

"Yep.
Definitely time to go."

THE PUNCHLINE

Why? What just happened?

THE SET-UP

The burnt-out employee

"This looks like a job for..."

THE PUNCHLINE

"Definitely someone else instead of me."

THE SET-UP

"Imma tell you one more time, and then we're just gonna have to fight."

THE PUNCHLINE

Well, that escalated quickly. Or did it? What has led to this moment? What happens next?

THE SET-UP

"That attitude?

Just put it on the bottom of your shoe and walk on it.."

THE PUNCHLINE

Well, dang. Doesn't get more blunt and heartless than that.
Who is on the receiving end of this?
What did they do to deserve it?

THE SET-UP

A car drives by, and in the driver's seat is...

THE PUNCHLINE

THE SET-UP

A boyfriend underestimates the rigor of cheerleading and bets his girlfriend that he can do it.

THE PUNCHLINE

Buddy should've thought about this a bit longer...

THE SET-UP
Every dog has her day

Not trusting her CEO husband, an insecure wife secretly infiltrates his headquarters by interviewing for and landing the head role in HR. Then she begins to vet out any pretty women.

THE PUNCHLINE
The women who at first happily accepted their role, when they find out the true reason why, they...

THE SET-UP

Someone completely disregards office politics to a hilarious degree — and outcome.

THE PUNCHLINE

THE SET-UP

Office politics and corporate culture go to new levels when something like a Big Brother streaming series sweeps through a major city's largest business district, putting all of the CEOs in one corporate house together.

THE PUNCHLINE
May the best win. And what exactly is the prize?

THE SET-UP

A woman accidentally mistakes the place of her interview and randomly sits down in a restaurant at the table of a man awaiting a blind date.

THE PUNCHLINE

Both unknowingly mistaking the other for someone they aren't places the woman in the most awkward intimate 'interview' she's ever had.

THE SET-UP

Two gym rats somehow start up a random, silent Crossfit competition that gets ridiculously wild.

THE PUNCHLINE

THE SET-UP

One Chicago man of partying yesteryears starts on a mission to bring house music back.

THE PUNCHLINE

THE SET-UP

A baby takes their first steps. But not to their parents.

THE PUNCHLINE

And not uncoordinated and wobbly like normal babies. Instead, they have perfect strides — and other plans where they want to take them. They're headed to...

THE SET-UP

A baby doesn't play about their lunch time. And so, the parents have to learn the hard way.

THE PUNCHLINE

THE SET-UP

While her friends are celebrating their first child or first-ever marriage proposal, a thirty-year-old celebrates her first...

THE PUNCHLINE

THE SET-UP

A woman, after getting the official diagnosis from her doctor, decides it calls for a proper party.

THE PUNCHLINE

What is the diagnosis? What is the party? Should it *really* be celebrated?

THE SET-UP

A theme park character tries to prank a kid during a family trip.

THE PUNCHLINE

The character quickly regrets their action.

THE SET-UP

Tell a story of a psychic and something they didn't even see coming in their own life.

THE PUNCHLINE

THE SET-UP

"If I don't make it back out..."

THE PUNCHLINE

"Tell your wife I love her."

THE SET-UP

While his friends are celebrating their first Harley, first son, or first promotion, a thirty-year-old celebrates his first-ever...

THE PUNCHLINE

THE SET-UP

"If you blink, you'll miss it!!"

THE PUNCHLINE

"Whew. Good thing I blinked."

THE SET-UP

Parents with a stubborn kid who doesn't want to eat anything but pizza decide to give it to him every single night for dinner.

THE PUNCHLINE

And for lunch and dinner on the weekends.

THE SET-UP

A psychic running a money laundering scheme dashes by, with informants right on her tail.

THE PUNCHLINE

"Well...looks like she didn't see THAT coming."

THE SET-UP

A spiritual coach has a mega-tantrum during their streaming hosted virtual retreat on their social media page.

THE PUNCHLINE

None of the retreat attendees are afraid. But they are entertained...and screen recording the entire thing.

THE SET-UP

A cross-examination between an expert witness and a prosecutor gets pretty feisty.

THE PUNCHLINE

THE SET-UP
Gen Z dating problems

A jaded social influencer quickly becomes more jaded when she discovers that non-social media guys are just like social media ones.

THE PUNCHLINE

THE SET-UP
"I don't get paid enough for this."

A teacher steps out, leaving the pre-K class to fend for themselves.

THE PUNCHLINE

THE SET-UP

When someone discovers that the cause of their gastrointestinal pain isn't severe digestive problems but hairball problems, things go from strange to stranger.

THE PUNCHLINE

THE SET-UP

"Im sorry for what I said to you when I was freezing."

THE PUNCHLINE

THE SET-UP

"They say, 'Feed 'em long enough, they start to look like you.'"

THE PUNCHLINE

"Yeah, looks like that failed. So now, plan B: paternity test."

THE SET-UP

A man finds a genie who can grant any wish that makes his little heart content.

"Except THAT one."

THE PUNCHLINE

What is the one wish not happening for the poor guy in the immediate future? Will he ditch the genie and find another one? Should he check Craigslist?

THE SET-UP

The all-time grand internet hacker turns out to be a five-year-old whiz.

THE PUNCHLINE

THE SET-UP

"If your hands sound like sandpaper when you rub them together, yeah, that's a problem."

THE PUNCHLINE

THE SET-UP

"Why are you laughing?"

THE PUNCHLINE

"You'll NEVER guess what just happened! There..."

THE SET-UP

"Tomatoes have seeds. So...
How are they a vegetable?"

THE PUNCHLINE

"You know? You are so smart.
Yet so dumb."

THE SET-UP

"Mom, you got an F."

A mother prides herself on helping her son with his math homework the night before. Until he walks in with the returned homework and places it on her office table.

THE PUNCHLINE

THE SET-UP

"If she goes up any more, we might have to get the plunger."

THE PUNCHLINE

...

HUNH????

THE SET-UP

Divers expect long-anticipated gold at the bottom of a sinking desert deadpool. Instead, they find...

THE PUNCHLINE

THE SET-UP

Pick one:
-A woman who discovers her first-time gray hair at a time and place that isn't her home.
-A man who discovers his first-time bald spot during a first date or another time and place that isn't at home.

THE PUNCHLINE

When do they realize it? How do they realize it? Does someone let them know? How do they let them know? What happens then?

THE SET-UP

"Something's gotta give!"

THE PUNCHLINE

"Well, definitely won't be my pockets.
I'm stretching my cash 'til payday."

THE SET-UP

"How fast does this thing go?"

THE PUNCHLINE

"To behind bars at the speed of a red light if you go any faster."

THE SET-UP

A daughter pulls her father into a social media dance challenge. But then it kinda becomes a thing when they become instant viral stars from it.

THE PUNCHLINE

Then Dad gets big-headed.
And Daughter isn't goin' for that.

THE SET-UP

When you gotta go, you gotta go.
Even at work.

"How long you gonna be in there?"

THE PUNCHLINE

"Not sure. Depends on what you're offering as the better hourly rate."

THE SET-UP

A dog.
A ransom.
A will.

THE PUNCHLINE

And a bellhop who now has way more than he asked for on his shift.

THE SET-UP

A middle-aged man is determined to be the next Karate Kid.

THE PUNCHLINE

THE SET-UP

Slap Your Boss Day becomes a legal act across the world.

THE PUNCHLINE

BUT with one twist....

THE SET-UP

"How many times do I have to tell you? I-!"

THE PUNCHLINE

"Well, currently, it's been five. But I'd prefer eight. It's my favorite number."

THE SET-UP

"Are you really about to sit there and eat all of that?"

THE PUNCHLINE

"Are you really about to sit there and watch me to find out?
Otherwise, it's a pointless question, no?"

THE SET-UP
"What questions do you have for us?"

A candidate gets passive aggressively berated by interviewer's for being late to the video conference call. Little do they know, the candidate was told by the recruiter via email that the interviewers just arrived two minutes ago themselves.

THE PUNCHLINE

So the candidate dishes the attitude right back. Needless to say, they don't get that job at the end. But what *we* get is a crazy story in the middle of it.. Tell it.

THE SET-UP

"So, you want to have your cake and eat it too?"

THE PUNCHLINE

"Well, I'd prefer fried Twinkies, but since I'm already on the hook with this cheat day, I better just keep cool."

THE SET-UP

"I'm gonna count to ten. And when I open my eyes again, you better be that coat of tacky vomit-colored paint behind you on that wall."

THE PUNCHLINE

Who is this person speaking to? Why? And the larger question: Who really selected that tacky vomit color?

"Do you have another job lined up?"

"Nope.
BUT I HAVE THE DJ LOCKED IN!!"

THE PUNCHLINE

A man hosts a party to celebrate his termination.

Sometimes, being silent is much better than speaking.

THE PUNCHLINE

Yeah...A _____ at a _____ doesn't exactly follow that rule.

"We heard that you want to leave the team."

THE PUNCHLINE

"...Yay.
Your ears work."

THE SET-UP

"When are you gonna grow up?"

THE PUNCHLINE

"Around the same time you finally get out of your mother's basement."

THE SET-UP

"...You're muted..."

A manager immediately pulls an employee into a video call to berate him. But doesn't realize he hasn't toggled unmute until the end.

THE PUNCHLINE

THE SET-UP

When a stressed-out employee gets demanded by his boss to show his face at a mandatory 1-on-1 video call the following morning, he does.

THE PUNCHLINE

He brings his best face: a profile picture of...

THE SET-UP

A bootleg caterer places an order at a fast food drive-thru window.

THE PUNCHLINE

THE SET-UP

"Back in MY day..."

In order to get on their tablets, play on the internet, and make social media videos, a grandparent who's had enough makes the grandchildren pass *his* game: 1950s Jeopardy.

THE PUNCHLINE

"And the loser has to go outside. And take the trash with you."

THE SET-UP

Why did the employee cross the road?

"To get to the HR office they'd been eying from their twice-a-week desk office's window the past twelve months, only for them to find out their 'competitive' salary was like my 'raise' this past year."

THE PUNCHLINE

Welp. That grass was definitely not greener.

THE SET-UP

A man refuses to accept the fact that the '70s was the '70s fifty years ago.

THE PUNCHLINE

THE SET-UP

An American was born and raised in America — but from the time of childhood has voluntarily only watched European television, films, and music shows.

THE PUNCHLINE

THE SET-UP

Suddenly and inexplicably, all of the jingles, slang, and sayings ever known in history erase from history.

THE PUNCHLINE

And so, naturally, the world declares a pandemic.

THE SET-UP

"The last time this happened, we..."

THE PUNCHLINE

THE SET-UP

A reluctantly retired ventriloquist and young girl who loves dolls become pals. Then he meets her grandmother who has automatonophobia.

THE PUNCHLINE

THE SET-UP

Should've spent more time on that "doctors near me" Internet search

"Just shut it off then shut if back on."

THE PUNCHLINE

"...This is about my constipation..."

THE SET-UP

"Turn left."   "Then make a slight left."   "And then you're
"Unh-hunh."   "Unh-hunh."   there, okay?"
"Turn right."   "And then look right."   "Nope."
"Unh-hunh."   "Okay."

THE PUNCHLINE

THE SET-UP

(Bares teeth at employee): "I don't get it, you come in everyday, sit, and don't talk to the team. You're clearly not here to make friends."

(Whistles with a pointer finger at manager): "You got it right, John. Uh-oh...Think that deserves some...PIZZA!"

THE PUNCHLINE

THE SET-UP

A fart is heard from across the world.

Which is essentially across the street for the one big step a giant takes after the one big gas emission.

THE PUNCHLINE

THE SET-UP

During a red traffic light, a family of geese slowly waddle through the lanes. A man hops out of his car and flaps his arms toward the geese to make them hurry up.

THE PUNCHLINE

We're too afraid to know what's goin' on in the man's head. So, instead, make us laugh with what the surrounding car drivers are thinking. Out loud.

THE SET-UP

A road crosses a street with a chicken.

THE PUNCHLINE

Yep. You read that right.

THE SET-UP

It is SO inappropriate, but your main character just can't stop doing it.

THE PUNCHLINE

What is 'it?'

THE SET-UP

A person who hasn't worn contact lenses in nearly a decade and their first day back into trying to put them in.

THE PUNCHLINE

THE SET-UP

A manager decides today is a good day to fill her small team in on her husband's possible erectile dysfunction after discovering a men's health subscription box in his medicine cabinet.

THE PUNCHLINE

THE SET-UP

A blind date goes a little something like this:

"So...
Tell me what excited you about this opportunity."

THE PUNCHLINE

Explain what the other person says next? And then? And THEN? How does it all end?

THE SET-UP

A broken crayon
A crying kid
A teen, their phone, their social media live record...that can only mean one thing...

THE PUNCHLINE

THE SET-UP

An employee goes to HR about the sexual harassment they're getting...from HR.

THE PUNCHLINE

THE SET-UP

A stuffed animal
A person with ludilophobia

THE PUNCHLINE

THE SET-UP

Two longtime senior-aged friends get into yet another debate on sports and politics.

THE PUNCHLINE

However, today is not the right day, the debate intensifying during the most inappropriate time when all around them...

THE SET-UP

"You see this right here?
That's your brain on stupid."

THE PUNCHLINE

THE SET-UP

"You all's generation think you're saying something new, and you're really not sayin' ----"

THE PUNCHLINE

THE SET-UP

"I have a confession to make."

THE PUNCHLINE

"I'm really a..."

THE SET-UP
I Mom, 2 Many Kids,
I Approaching Kid Entertainment Center

"Mommy, mom! When we walk in, CAN WE——!?"

THE PUNCHLINE

"Yeah. Unh-huh. Come on. Get in."

THE SET-UP

"I GIVE UP!!"

THE PUNCHLINE

"...
About time."

THE SET-UP

A mother and a son disagree on his girlfriend's cooking.

THE PUNCHLINE

And that, folks, is how World War III started.

THE SET-UP

It's time for yet another family barbecue with the emergence of yet a new summer.

THE PUNCHLINE

And Uncle has gotten ahold of yet another Jack Daniel's...

THE SET-UP

Introduce the family.
Where everyone in it is named after _____.

THE PUNCHLINE

Having enough, a mom disappears from home for the weekend and sets off to...

"What do you want to be when you grow up?"

"Good question. I'll let you know when I make it there."

Two strangers keep awkwardly meeting up in the same aisles in a grocery store.

But with an unexpected catch.

THE SET-UP

A fed-up couple, to whom all of the extended family comes to for help, and the sabbatical they decide to take as a result.

THE PUNCHLINE

THE SET-UP

You don't have to go home, but you ARE leaving this one.

A couple, a day after their hosted family Thanksgiving weekend, kick everyone out to go celebrate their anniversary.

THE PUNCHLINE

"You don't have to go home, but WE'RE going to Kauai!"

THE SET-UP

Clean up on aisle "Why did I decide to have children again?"

As one kid lets it rip from the front end, the other lets it rip from the back.

THE PUNCHLINE

THE SET-UP

As kids on college break come through the front door, their parents sneak out through the garage.

THE PUNCHLINE

THE SET-UP

A guy gets a little too ambitious at the gym.

THE PUNCHLINE

THE SET-UP

"Okay, so I don't have enough time to explain this, but—When you get in, DON'T look up. Because..."

THE PUNCHLINE

So, naturally, we look up. And what do we see?

THE SET-UP

A hunter realizes sticking his head into a rabbit hole is a bad idea...after he's stuck his head into the rabbit hole.

THE PUNCHLINE

THE SET-UP

A man stages a kidnapping to get back at his wife.

THE PUNCHLINE

Except his wife already knows.

THE SET-UP

A defense witness who goes up to the stand doesn't really do a good job at being a defense witness.

THE PUNCHLINE

THE SET-UP

A remote employee's cat keeps making guest appearances during a video meeting.

THE PUNCHLINE

THE SET-UP

The standard friends to lovers trope.

THE PUNCHLINE

But with a twist.

THE SET-UP

The standard enemies to lovers trope.

THE PUNCHLINE
But with a twist.

THE SET-UP

"Yep, that's me. And I know you're probably wondering how I got here..."

THE PUNCHLINE

Tell the story of a dog's cone of shame through the dog's mind.

THE SET-UP

Siri and a driver get into a battle of choice words during a route gone wrong.

THE PUNCHLINE

THE SET-UP

After a long day, work included, an increasingly frustrated and hangry driver vocalizes their every moment of the ride and traffic.

THE PUNCHLINE

THE SET-UP

An ATM and a busy bank customer have two different sets of plans.

THE PUNCHLINE

THE SET-UP

A kid's first meeting with Santa doesn't exactly go how *any*one planned.

THE PUNCHLINE

THE SET-UP

A long-standing shopper's initially excited experience with the fresh self-checkout section of an older grocery store quickly loses its luster.

THE PUNCHLINE

When...

THE SET-UP

Santa asks a kid at the shopping mall if he's been good that year. He looks at his parents, looks back at Santa, then spills all of his secret indiscretions (including stealing candy!). Then, of course, he starts crying.

THE PUNCHLINE

THE SET-UP

Older siblings take on disguises and (not-so-inconspicuously) follow their baby sibling's first date for the entire evening.

THE PUNCHLINE

And if that all seems as unsuccessful as it all sounds, you're right.

THE SET-UP

A horticulturalist decides to become a barber. Because what's the difference between cutting literal bushes and cutting bushes of hair?

THE PUNCHLINE

THE SET-UP

A forty-year-old man is determined to fulfill his unfulfilled dream of becoming a bull rider. Without having a lick of experience...And **NOTHING** can stop him.
Not even common sense.

THE PUNCHLINE

THE SET-UP

A man decides to get even with his savage next-door neighbords: two eight-year-old brothers.

THE PUNCHLINE

THE SET-UP

An inept landscaper.
A residential gig.
A pile of hidden cash.
And the neighborhood watch: a 75-year-old widow.

THE PUNCHLINE

THE SET-UP

A German Shepherd.
A hand.
A prank.

THE PUNCHLINE
A prank where the real joke is on the owner.

THE SET-UP

In a family of clowns, one has other plans.

THE PUNCHLINE
Plans to become a...

THE SET-UP

An employee quickly discovers their imposter syndrome is real.

THE PUNCHLINE
Oh. No.

THE SET-UP

Document the everyday crazy encounters of a retail employee.

THE PUNCHLINE

THE SET-UP

A recruiter looks over the employment history of an applicant and discovers something bizarre.

THE PUNCHLINE

One of the recent 'jobs' is...

THE SET-UP

"Can you give me a reason for this gap in your employment?"

THE PUNCHLINE

"Sure. Which fake version do you want? I have three of them that I rotate."

THE SET-UP

"What do you like to do for fun?"

THE PUNCHLINE
"You REALLY don't want to know the answer to that."

THE SET-UP

"How do you just drop people like that?"

THE PUNCHLINE
"Well, first it starts with dropping them off your Following list."

THE SET-UP

"Who invited *her*?"

THE PUNCHLINE

"Who invited YOU??"

THE SET-UP

A shopper comes across a buy one, get one free deal.
But it's not exactly a usual kind of deal.

THE PUNCHLINE

Let's just say it's...

THE SET-UP

A worn-out mom of highly energetic twins takes to the
social media streets. She joins an online marketplace
and posts this: Buy one, get one free.

THE PUNCHLINE

However, one of the twins is thirty years older than the other...

THE SET-UP

A brainiac suddenly awakens with a loss of all of their
intelligence. Needless to say, hysteria ensues.

THE PUNCHLINE

Desperate, the former brainiac...

THE SET-UP

A mechanic runs up against one vehicle that is just determined not to be fixed.

THE PUNCHLINE

THE SET-UP

"Who made this?"

THE PUNCHLINE

"Why? You plannin' on taking the recipe so yours can actually taste good?"

THE SET-UP

A social media challenge.
A hairless cat.
A law office.
A viral conspiracy.

THE PUNCHLINE

After inhaling a large amount of dust during a furnace cleanup, an **HVAC** tech has the superpower of...

THE PUNCHLINE

A secret shopper gets a **VERY** weird request.

THE PUNCHLINE

A secret shopper.
A blackmail.
A cat.
A house rental.

THE PUNCHLINE

THE SET-UP

Tomatoes that look like their own diet is steroids.
A guy actually on steroids.
An agrochemical and agricultural biotechnology corporation.

THE PUNCHLINE

THE SET-UP

A grandma isn't so hard of hearing as she portrays.

THE PUNCHLINE

The truth comes to light when...

THE SET-UP

A grandpa isn't so inept at technology and computers as he portrays. He just uses his grandchildren because he's lazy.

THE PUNCHLINE

And also because...

Someone is reading aloud instructions but abruptly stops because...

THE PUNCHLINE

"She looks JUST like you!!"

A woman awakens to find that her teen daughter who favors her has literally become her mini-me: herself as a teen.

THE PUNCHLINE

And if that all seems as torturous (for all in the home) as it all sounds, you're right.

THE SET-UP

A concert attendee out for her birthday isn't ready when the music artists call her up on the stage.

THE PUNCHLINE

What happens next?

THE SET-UP

A dogsitter is up for a wild day.

THE PUNCHLINE

What starts off as a normal visit to the dog park turns into...

THE SET-UP

An introvert decides to go out for the night and slowly realizes she made a very. bad. decision.

THE PUNCHLINE

THE SET-UP

A poet decides to try a hand at rap.

THE PUNCHLINE

It's all just rhyming words and metaphors, right? (RIGHT?)

THE SET-UP

After winning a contest to be a band's personal assistant for the day, the fan, needless to say, soon becomes an ex-fan.

THE PUNCHLINE

THE SET-UP

A shoe clerk puts a heel onto the real-life Cinderella of modern day.

THE PUNCHLINE

And of course, immediately, Cinderella runs off. And the clerk runs after her, saying, "Hey, you have to pay for that!" And THEN...

THE SET-UP

A new car salesman who hasn't had a sale yet (and really should choose another profession) almost closes on a deal. But then, of course, he messes up by...

THE PUNCHLINE

THE SET-UP

A playgirl and a playboy start to develop feelings for each other. And panic.

THE PUNCHLINE

THE SET-UP

Two social influencers have respectively met their match.

THE PUNCHLINE

THE SET-UP

A playgirl and a playboy meet their match in each other.

THE PUNCHLINE

THE SET-UP

An internet social justice warrior.
A vlogger journalist.
A mistaken identity.
A bribe gone completely wrong.
A family reunion park gathering.

THE PUNCHLINE

Where is this all going?

THE SET-UP

A tragic attempt at 'artwork.'
A new cryptocurrency.
A press release.
A pet rabbit that always goes nuts.

THE PUNCHLINE

How do they all fit together?

THE SET-UP

A shed.
An old bag of chips.
A self-professed Plant Whisperer.

THE PUNCHLINE

THE SET-UP

An astrologer with a blog.
A Cadillac.
A group of people angry about their reading not coming true.

THE PUNCHLINE

A Benz pulls up and...

THE SET-UP

A very determined soup eater.
An electric can opener.
And an equally determined coup can set on not being opened.

THE PUNCHLINE

THE SET-UP

A person is going about their regular day, about their regular business when someone else's business involuntarily becomes their business.

THE PUNCHLINE

How? What happens next?

THE SET-UP

As a neighborhood resident is on the sidewalk, a car zips up, throws out a box, emits the sounds of crazed laughter, then zips off.

THE PUNCHLINE

What does the person do next?

THE SET-UP

A parent catches their child sticking their tongue out at their grandmother behind the back.

THE PUNCHLINE

What is the child's fate looking like?

THE SET-UP

One high schooler.
One teacher.
One week of detentions.

THE PUNCHLINE

THE SET-UP

Catnip.
Cats.
Enough said.

THE PUNCHLINE

THE SET-UP

A financial aid representative.
A college office.
And an enrolling student who just ain't gettin' it. None of it.

THE PUNCHLINE

THE SET-UP

A family's wild experience on a new cruise line that's just debutted.

THE PUNCHLINE

They get on the ship and quickly realize the cruise isn't...

THE SET-UP

A cop goes on a wild chase after a car, finally pins it, approaches the car, and realizes it's a self-driving car.

THE PUNCHLINE

THE SET-UP
"Ma'am, I'll need to see some ID."

A woman who is truly of age
and a store clerk who just ain't buyin' it.

THE PUNCHLINE

THE SET-UP
Sneakerhead

A sneaker fanatic literally becomes a person with a sneaker for a head as punishment for...

THE PUNCHLINE

THE SET-UP

An accountant's first day on the job includes accidentally giving an employee six figures of a paycheck into their checking account.

THE PUNCHLINE

Needless to say, the customer goes into hiding and...

THE SET-UP

A vegan has no idea about the mental scarring they're getting themselves into when they decide to web search how honey is made.

THE PUNCHLINE

THE SET-UP

A person who is easily offended by everything meets a person who is easily annoyed by everything. This might be the greatest test of patience for both of them.

THE PUNCHLINE

Do either of them make it out alive? Or do they go insane first?

THE SET-UP

Someone doesn't get the memo about the dress code to an event. But they sure understand when they walk in...

THE PUNCHLINE

THE SET-UP

What starts out as a normal event assignment for a food caterer suddenly becomes the wildest night of their life.

THE PUNCHLINE

THE SET-UP

A makeup artist doesn't realize the services they'll provide for a new client is to fake a...

THE PUNCHLINE

THE SET-UP

Aspiring burglars run up into a social influencer's home —
only to find that it's an entire manufactured set.

THE PUNCHLINE

THE SET-UP

An aspiring lawyer (still in high school) takes a class mock
trial a little too seriously.

THE PUNCHLINE

THE SET-UP

The oldest child in a family watches their siblings for the
night for the first time ever when their parents go on a
weekend trip.

THE PUNCHLINE
What happens? Do they all have two eyes, ears, hands, and
feet still intact when the parents return?

THE SET-UP

An audience is loving a singer.

THE PUNCHLINE

Until one off-key note.

THE SET-UP

A very social media-active athlete
overly markets his skills.

THE PUNCHLINE

So, his followers proposition him to put his money where his mouth is.

THE SET-UP

A friend with a tendency to cling
A pile of horse manure
A carnival

THE PUNCHLINE

THE SET-UP

A person suddenly can only express tears for happiness and laughter for anger.

THE PUNCHLINE

What do they express for amusement?

THE SET-UP

A summer backyard bean bag toss game gets serious as if money is on the line.

THE PUNCHLINE

THE SET-UP

Everything runs amok at a home daycare.

THE PUNCHLINE

THE SET-UP

A camera shy guy one day ends up in accidental photo bombs, video cameras, and social media background appearances wherever he goes.

THE PUNCHLINE

THE SET-UP

The latest family BBQ poker game gets testy once again.

THE PUNCHLINE

THE SET-UP

The 'family secrets unveiled at a family reunion' trope. But made ridiculous to the highest degree.

THE PUNCHLINE

THE SET-UP

A person awakens to discover that they can only move in a backward motion.

THE PUNCHLINE

People mistake it for a latest goofy internet challenge. But that's the least of this person's worries because...

THE SET-UP

Married to the job

A guy is so obsessed with his job that he literally wakes up to it as his wife and with his real wife nowhere in sight.

THE PUNCHLINE

THE SET-UP

A class of kindergarteners scare every single teacher away.

THE PUNCHLINE

Until they finally meet their match.

A group of teenage grandchildren think they can take advantage of their grandparents during one summer vacation stay.

THE PUNCHLINE

Welp, they thought wrong.

Mad at his coach, a goalie purposely doesn't block a single shot from the opposing team.

THE PUNCHLINE

Mad at his coach, a power forward posterizes the entire game — on his own teammates.

THE PUNCHLINE

THE SET-UP

A day is going well for your character...when THIS happens.

THE PUNCHLINE

THE SET-UP

An IT specialist leaves a little surprise within everyone's computers on the day of his termination.

THE PUNCHLINE

But he saves the best one for...

THE SET-UP

A person scared of everything.
A person who claims no fears.
A stuck elevator.

THE PUNCHLINE

THE SET-UP

The roof. THE ROOF!!

During a sudden needed repair at a house party, an electrician sets the roof on fire.

THE PUNCHLINE

Literally.

THE SET-UP

A catnapper runs across the wrong family.

THE PUNCHLINE

More specifically: the wrong daughter in the family.

THE SET-UP

Kids prank call the wrong person.

THE PUNCHLINE

THE SET-UP

A hopeful carjacker runs across the wrong car owner.

THE PUNCHLINE
And car.

THE SET-UP

A fed-up coach goes (comically) OFF on his players.

THE PUNCHLINE

How do they react?

THE SET-UP

"Sometimes I wonder what it would've been like if that had never happened.

...Ya know?"

THE PUNCHLINE
"We both wouldn't be here: You'd be in a cemetery, and I'd be in a prison cell. That's what."

THE SET-UP

A state trooper's first day on the highway is eventful, to say the least.

THE PUNCHLINE

THE SET-UP

When a group of cousins reunite for a summer trip, they are in for a wild next couple of days. All thanks to one of the cousins in the bunch.

THE PUNCHLINE

It all starts off with a car cutting in front of them on the way to their house rental.

THE SET-UP

An international flight gets pretty crazy. It's going to be a long fourteen hours.

THE PUNCHLINE

Or maybe even more.

THE SET-UP

A group of kids want to act a fool, and an older family relative says they got time today for it.

THE PUNCHLINE

THE SET-UP

A usually laidback uncle suddenly storms upstairs with a Terrible Two toddler nephew and has a few words for him. With everyone else stopping dead in their tracks.

THE PUNCHLINE

THE SET-UP

One morning.
One kid.
One uneaten bowl of oatmeal.
One humbled dad.

THE PUNCHLINE

THE SET-UP

A group of residents in a nursing home have enough and decide it's time to cause a riot.

THE PUNCHLINE

THE SET-UP

A prank war starts between residents and caretakers in a senior living facility.

THE PUNCHLINE

THE SET-UP

The parents of Pee Wee kids on two opposing teams get into their own match.

THE PUNCHLINE

THE SET-UP

The roller rink days of a group of skaters who don't realize it's no longer 1972.

THE PUNCHLINE

THE SET-UP

A self-driving car is on the run, leading a hot pursuit chase.

THE PUNCHLINE

THE SET-UP

If a store clerk was asking for a quick end to their boredom (and shift/work day), they now have their wish granted...

THE PUNCHLINE

...when a pig-masked person comes galloping right at the cash register. Yes, galloping.

THE SET-UP

Two people first meet through two mutual matchmaking friends...

THE PUNCHLINE

And respectively fall in love at first sight. With the other's friend instead.

THE SET-UP

A gas station employee notices a customer doing the weirdest things at his car.

THE PUNCHLINE

None of which includes actually getting gas.

THE SET-UP

A manager during an offsite team lunch meeting decides it's a good time to let one of the team members know about how their job was almost their other team member's instead.

THE PUNCHLINE

The team member sitting right beside them.

THE SET-UP

During what was supposed to be an intimate dinner, one of the individuals in the argumentative relationship decides, while taking a bite of crab cakes, that now is a good time to stick their fork in the other's eye.

THE PUNCHLINE

THE SET-UP

Waste management professionals of garbarge collection discover a load of cash. And subsequent arguing over the money is just the start of their day of events.

THE PUNCHLINE

THE SET-UP

A group of kids sending each other answers to a test in class don't realize the teacher is aware of it all.

THE PUNCHLINE

THE SET-UP

Happy birthday to you, dear cousin.
Happy birthday to you!

Long lost cousins decide now is a good time as any to celebrate all of their birthdays from the past to catch up on old and lost times.

THE PUNCHLINE

ALL of the birthdays.

THE SET-UP

A day of talent show auditions at a community college is very entertaining, to say the least.

THE PUNCHLINE

THE SET-UP

A young two-year-old excites her parents and all of their internet followers with her good vocabulary.

THE PUNCHLINE

But maybe it's *too* good...

THE SET-UP

Turns out Santa doesn't offer such a great benefits package.

THE PUNCHLINE

What happens next? Looks like Santa needs an HR rep and...

THE SET-UP

A woman seems to be picture perfect to a guy.

Except for ONE thing...

THE PUNCHLINE

THE SET-UP

A hairstylist makes a big "Whoops" in a client's hair.

THE PUNCHLINE

Does (or when does) the client realize? Does the client then give a big "Whoops" to the hairstylist's face to return the favor? What does the hairstylist do then?

THE SET-UP

"Great. One's an 'astrologer,' one is 'plant-based,' and the last is both. This is gonna be an interesting night."

THE PUNCHLINE

Who is this person speaking? Who are they speaking about? How come they don't sound excited? How does the night pan out?

THE SET-UP

A video game fanatic's matchup with a computer-generated opponent online gets more and more bizarre as the opponent starts dishing back the jabs and choice of words.

THE PUNCHLINE

THE SET-UP

A kid isn't feeling his Christmas gifts and, therefore, decides Santa needs to hear a few words on his official social media page.

THE PUNCHLINE

(Yes. Santa @TheNorthPole has a social media page.)

THE SET-UP

Santa is looking for new elves (It's a long anti-work story. Yes, even at The North Pole.).

THE PUNCHLINE

So, he goes to the internet job boards. Except no one takes the job listing seriously. Like, come on. Santa isn't just posting online...Right???

THE SET-UP

He's making a list...and realizing he's on it.

Santa himself gets put on the Naughty List for...

THE PUNCHLINE

THE SET-UP

Did you know The Tooth Fairy has kids?

THE PUNCHLINE

Welp. Now it's time to fill in the rest of the world. And it turns out, to the world's additional surprise, that the kids are...

THE SET-UP
Awk-warrrrrrrd

Two guys start off laughing hysterically. Until they realize neither of them said or did anything funny...

THE PUNCHLINE
Then they turn around to see someone laughing tears and pointing at them. Because...

THE SET-UP

Someone decides to break into the wrong house.

THE PUNCHLINE
Quite literally. And now this robber's in for the night of their life.

THE SET-UP

A first date...and a fart escapes.

THE PUNCHLINE

Write to Keep On Crying

(TEARS!)

& CREW

Write to Keep On (Keeping On): Writing Story Prompts for a Coming-of-Age, Love Story, and More Drama

Write to Keep On Flying: Writing Story Prompts for an Out-of-This-World Adventure or Other Children's Novel, Screenplay, or Stageplay

Write to Keep Them Guessing and Excited: Writing Story Prompts for a Provoking Sci-Fi, Fantasy, Thriller/Mystery, or Action Novel, Screenplay, or Stageplay

By Hakeela Buford
Here on Amazon

AF.FORD media.co